MAGNIFICENT MOLDS

RECIPES FOR MAKE-AHEAD MAGIC

Nancy Fair McIntyre

Illustrations by Maxwell Moray

Cobble & Mickle Books
Portland, Oregon

Published by Cobble & Mickle Books, P.O. Box 6533, Portland, Oregon 97228

Cover Design by Margot Thompson, Portland, Oregon

Printed in the United States of America
You may order single copies of this book direct from the publisher for $7.95 plus $1.50 postage and handling.

Other Cobble & Mickle cookbook titles:
4 & 20 Blackbirds, Cooking in Crust by Nancy Fair McIntyre
Terra Cotta Cuisine, Recipes for Pottery Cookware by Nancy Fair McIntyre
Great Convertibles, 7 Master Recipes for Superb Dishes from Appetizers to Entrees to Desserts by Kit Snedaker
Michael Grant's Cookbook, Hearty Fare From a Country Kitchen by Michael Grant

Library of Congress Catalog Card Number 90-90-82550
ISBN 0-9616524-7-0

Table of Contents

The molded dish is a work of art you can eat! It dazzles the eye, tempts the palate and pays tribute to you, the artist in the kitchen. Today's busy cooks know these tasty dishes require little artistry to produce. All of which make molded foods a smart choice for entertaining.

We give you a collection of the world's most beautiful chilled specialties made with fresh ingredients that take minimal preparation time. Seasonal produce, fresh herbs, succulent seafood and meats are delicately suspended in an easy-to-master basic aspic recipe. Flavored with wine or cream and spices, exciting molded entrees become the focal point for your meal. Nothing keeps a dinner on ice as long or as well as these refrigerated foods. Prepare them hours ahead, or even better, the day before. They're ready to unmold and serve anytime you're ready—a real boon to dual-career couples and active families. On the following pages you'll find complete instructions and helpful directions for unmolding dishes.

In choosing a mold, be adventurous and cast your culinary talents in a variety of designs and fanciful forms. Fresh, nourishing and colorful, molded dishes are limited only by your imagination. So let yourself go and have some fun with make-ahead magic—there's no end of culinary surprises you can turn out.

Molded dishes must unmold perfectly down to the last quivering curlicue—or all is lost. Failures are impossible to camouflage in this art. However, the rules for molded cookery are easy; and if you follow these basic steps you'll get perfect results.

In using unflavored gelatin it is necessary to first soften the gelatin powder in cold water or cold liquid and then dissolve it in hot water or liquid as per directions in all recipes. Flavored gelatin, however, need not be softened first in cold liquid.

Be sure the gelatin mixture is cooled to the point where it's slightly thicker than the consistency of unbeaten egg white before combining it with various ingredients. This helps your dish to gel more quickly in the mold. To hasten the cooling process, put the gelatin mixture in a bowl nestled in ice.

Keep mold and all utensils icy cold before using. Molds should be lightly but thoroughly greased to facilitate easy unmolding. It is also wise to rinse a mold in cold water as a wet mold is recommended in many recipes.

In instances where an aspic glaze is used on the bottom of the mold, or throughout the mold, decorations and other ingredients must be placed in various designs between layers of aspic. It is important that each coating of aspic completely gels in the refrigerator before adding another layer of ingredients.

Allow at least four to six hours for a mold to set—even longer if it's a large mold. Overnight gelling is best if you have the time.

To unmold, dip the bottom of the mold in hot water for a few seconds. Or, soak a dish towel in hot water, wring it out and place around the mold for a few seconds.

Invert a chilled, wet serving plate over the mold and quickly turn both upside down. (The wet plate enables the molded dish to slide out more readily onto the plate.) When the mold is inverted, give the bottom and sides a light, sharp tap to help loosen the contents. If the aspic still clings, dip the mold in hot water again or wrap it in a hot towel for a few seconds. With some molds it's also good to first run the tip of a knife around the inside edges to loosen the contents.

Once your dish is unmolded, keep it chilled in the refrigerator until the last possible moment before serving. In the case of a large dinner party where you may be serving more than one mold, leave the reserve on ice to keep chilled and firm.

Recipes herein vary in quantity and should be multiplied or divided according to your needs and the dimensions of your mold or molds. Ordinarily 1 quart of aspic is sufficient for four people, however, it really depends on whether you're serving it as a side dish or entree. An easy way to measure the capacity of a mold is to count the cups of water it holds. In measuring gelatin, 1 Tbsp equals 1 package of unflavored gelatin.

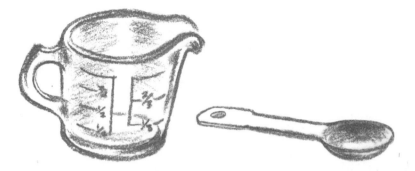

Aspic is merely a clear gelatin that is used in binding ingredients together in a mold. It is also used to coat cooked meats, poultry or fish, or as a sparkling garnish, when jellied and finely chopped. Aspics are made from homemade or commercial meat or chicken stocks combined with gelatin. They're often flavored with wine or tomato juice, or combined with mayonnaise or whipped cream. In the latter case the dish becomes a mousse.

For those who want to create their own aspic dishes, here's a quick, basic recipe for aspic:

4 1/2 tsp unflavored gelatin
1/3 cup water, beef or chicken stock, or dry white wine
2 10 1/2-oz cans beef or chicken consommé or equivalent in concentrated homemade stock.

Soften gelatin in cold water, cold stock or wine. Heat consomme to boiling point, remove from heat and stir in gelatin. Cool. Makes approximately 2 3/4 cups.

The stock or consommé used in making aspic should be of the same general base as the food used in the mold. In place of fish stock, which is often difficult to make, chicken stock may be used.

When making your own beef or chicken stock, be sure to skim off all fat when the stock has cooled. For each quart of cold stock, add 1 beaten egg white and 1 crumbled egg shell. Stir and heat to simmering point and simmer 15 minutes. Remove from stove and let stock stand 30 minutes. Strain through a cheesecloth wrung out in cold water.

It is interesting to note that the word aspic was believed to have come from the serpent, or asp, "where icy coldness recalls that of jelly." However, aspic more likely stems from the Greek word *aspis* which means buckler, or shield. The first molds were made in this form—as well as in the shape of a coiled snake.

GALA
ENTREES

Scotch Salmon Mousse

1 can (10 1/2 oz) tomato soup, undiluted
1 3-oz cream cheese, softened
2 Tbsp unflavored gelatin
1/2 cup cold water
1   1-lb can red salmon, drained and flaked
1/2 cup celery, diced
1/2 cup cucumbers, diced
1 cup mayonnaise
1 green pepper, diced
4 Tbsp green onions, minced
1 Tbsp Worcestershire sauce
1/2 tsp salt
1/8 tsp pepper

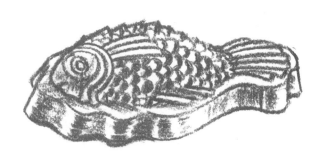

In the top of a double boiler, heat soup to boiling point. Add cream cheese and stir until it dissolves. Soften gelatin in cold water and add to soup and heat until it dissolves. Remove from stove and cool until mixture thickens. Add salmon, celery, cucumbers, mayonnaise, green pepper, green onions, Worcestershire, salt and pepper. Pour into mold and chill until firm.

Unmold and garnish with lemon wedges. Serves 6.

Poulet a l'Orange

1 1/2 Tbsp unflavored gelatin
1/2 cup cold orange juice
2 cups hot orange juice
1 navel orange, sectioned
1 1/2 Tbsp unflavored gelatin
2 Tbsp cold water
1 cup hot chicken stock
1 tsp salt
1/2 tsp white pepper
1 pimiento, chopped
1/2 tsp onion juice
3 cups diced cooked chicken, white
   meat only
1 cup heavy cream, whipped

Garnish: orange slices

Soften gelatin in cold orange juice, then dissolve in hot orange juice. Cool. Decorate the bottom of a mold with orange sections. Pour half the thickened orange juice over the top of the orange sections. Chill until firm.

Soften a second 1 1/2 Tbsp of gelatin in cold water and dissolve in hot chicken stock. Cool until it begins to thicken, and add salt, pepper, pimiento, onion juice and chicken. Fold in whipped cream. Pour over orange gelatin. Chill until firm. Pour the remaining orange gelatin over top and chill.

Garnish with orange slices. Serves 8.

3 lb shank of veal (with bone)
1 carrot
1 onion, sliced
2 bay leaves
1 Tbsp salt
1/4 tsp peppercorns
1 celery stalk
1/2 tsp basil
2 Tbsp unflavored gelatin
1 cup cold stock
3 cups hot stock
1 Tbsp parsley, chopped

Place veal in a large sauce pan with sufficient water to barely cover meat. Add carrot, onion, bay leaves, salt, peppercorns, celery and basil. Cover and bring to a boil. Simmer 2 hours or until meat is tender enough to fall off the bone. Strain broth, chill and skim off fat. Reserve 1 cup cold stock.

Boil remaining stock until it's reduced to 3 cups. Soften gelatin in cold stock, and dissolve in hot stock. Chill. Cut meat from bone, cut away any fat and cut into julienne strips. Cut vegetables into julienne strips. Fold veal and vegetables into stock together with chopped parsley. Pour into mold and chill until firm.

Serve with the following caper sauce:

3 Tbsp capers, drained
1 cup mayonnaise
1 Tbsp lemon juice
2 Tbsp chopped chives
1/4 tsp Tabasco

Combine capers with mayonnaise, lemon juice, chives and Tabasco. Serves 6.

Spinach Ring

6 packages of frozen chopped spinach, thawed
5 green onions, finely chopped
3 Tbsp chicken-seasoned stock base
1/2 tsp ground pepper
2 Tbsp unflavored gelatin
1/2 cup cold water
1 cup sour cream
3/4 cup celery, finely chopped
1/4 cup parsley, chopped
1 Tbsp herb seasoning
4 Tbsp vinegar
1/2 tsp ground pepper

In a saucepan, combine thawed chopped spinach, onions, chicken stock base and ground pepper. Cook according to directions on spinach package. Drain well. Soak gelatin in cold water and dissolve over hot water. Add gelatin to spinach and cool.

Combine sour cream, celery, parsley, herb seasoning, vinegar and ground pepper and stir into spinach mixture. Pack into a ring mold and chill until firm.

Unmold and serve with a sauce made from 1 cup sour cream combined with 3 Tbsp horseradish. Serves 12.

1   4-lb chicken
1 carrot
1 stalk celery
1 bay leaf
1 Tbsp salt
3 peppercorns
1 onion
6 cups chicken stock
4 Tbsp unflavored gelatin
1/2 cup cold water
2 Tbsp brandy
2 hard-cooked eggs, thinly sliced
2 cups canned baby peas, drained

Soften gelatin in cold water and dissolve in hot stock. Chill until stock begins to thicken. Stir in brandy.

Place chicken in a large pot with water to cover. Add carrot, celery, bay leaf, salt, peppercorns and onion. Cover and simmer for 1 1/2 hours or until chicken is very tender. Remove chicken. Skin and bone chicken, and cut into slices. Strain chicken stock and measure 6 cups.

Pour a thin layer of chicken stock on the bottom of a mold and chill. Arrange a layer of hard-cooked egg slices on top in a decorative pattern. Moisten with aspic and chill. Arrange a layer of chicken slices over the eggs, spoon over a little aspic and chill. Next, sprinkle a layer of canned peas over the chicken and spoon over more aspic. Repeat layers of chicken and peas with aspic between layers until mold is full. Chill until firm. Serves 8.

4 Tbsp unflavored gelatin
1/2 cup cold white wine
1 qt tomato juice
1 cup dry white wine
1 tsp salt
2 tsp brown sugar
4 whole cloves
6 thin onion slices
1 bay leaf
2 Tbsp lemon juice
1 1/2 cups crab meat, boned and flaked
1 cup celery, minced
2 Tbsp capers, chopped
1/3 cup black olives, chopped
3/4 cup mayonnaise

Garnish: chopped parsley

Soften gelatin in cold white wine. In a saucepan combine tomato juice, dry white wine, salt, brown sugar, cloves, onion slices and bay leaf. Bring to a boil and simmer 10 minutes. Strain and stir in gelatin-wine mixture. Add lemon juice. Cool until mixture begins to thicken. Pour into individual heart-shaped molds about 1 inch deep. Chill until firm.

In a bowl combine crab meat, celery, capers, olives and mayonnaise.

Unmold individual hearts on lettuce and spoon out a heaping tablespoon of crab salad on the center of each heart. Top with chopped parsley. Serves 10.

Lamb Mousse

2 cups cooked lamb, finely diced
1 1/2 cups lamb stock (or consommé)
3 egg yolks
1 1/2 Tbsp unflavored gelatin
1/4 cup cold water
1/2 tsp salt
1/4 tsp paprika
1/8 tsp cayenne
1 cup heavy cream, whipped
1/2 cup pecans, finely chopped

Garnish: pimiento slices, parsley

Soften gelatin in cold water and stir into hot custard mixture. Add salt, paprika, cayenne. Chill until custard begins to set and fold in whipped cream, pecans and lamb. Pour into mold and chill.

Unmold and garnish with pimiento strips and parsley. Serves 6.

Cut any fat from lamb, and finely dice meat. Combine lamb stock or consomme with beaten egg yolks and slowly cook in top of a double boiler until thickened.

2 Tbsp unflavored gelatin
1/4 cup cold chicken broth
3 cups hot chicken broth
1/2 tsp salt
1/2 tsp paprika
1   15-oz can asparagus tips (drained)
2 cups cooked lobster meat, boned and
     flaked

Garnish: watercress

Soften gelatin in cold chicken broth and dissolve in hot chicken broth. Chill until mixture begins to thicken. Coat ring mold with aspic and chill. Line mold with asparagus tips arranged in a decorative pattern, and spoon half of the aspic over asparagus. Chill.

Fill mold with lobster meat and add remaining aspic. Chill until firm.

Unmold and surround with watercress. Serve with mayonnaise combined with capers and chopped parsley. Serves 6.

1 1/2 Tbsp unflavored gelatin
2 cups cold chicken broth
1 cup cooked lobster meat, boned and
    flaked
1 cup cooked chicken, diced
1/2 cup cucumbers, diced and seeded
1/2 cup celery, diced
1 Tbsp lemon juice
1/2 tsp dry mustard
salt and pepper to taste

Soften gelatin in 1/4 cup cold chicken broth. Heat remaining broth to boiling point and add gelatin. Stir until dissolved. Chill broth until it begins to thicken; add lobster, chicken, cucumbers, celery, lemon juice, dry mustard and salt and pepper to taste. Pour into lobster mold and chill until firm.

Serve with 1 cup mayonnaise whipped together with 1 mashed avocado. Serves 6.

3   1/2 lb fresh halibut
2 cups white wine
2 cups cold water
1 bay leaf
1 sprig parsley
1 onion, chopped
1 carrot, thinly sliced
1/2 green pepper, seeded and chopped
1 leek (white part only), sliced
2 sprigs celery leaves
1/4 tsp thyme
1 clove garlic
4 peppercorns
3/4 tsp salt
2 egg shells
2 egg whites
2 Tbsp unflavored gelatin
3/4 cup cold water
2 Tbsp lemon juice
1/4 cup green pepper, chopped
2 Tbsp pimiento, chopped
2 Tbsp black olives, chopped
1 Tbsp parsley, chopped
1 Tbsp chives, chopped

Place halibut in a fish-poaching pan together with white wine, water, bay leaf, parsley, onion, carrot, green pepper, leek, celery leaves, thyme, garlic, peppercorns and salt. Simmer gently for 20 minutes until fish flakes easily. Remove fish and strain broth through double thickness of cheesecloth into another pan. Bring to a boil and clarify stock by adding egg shells and egg whites. Simmer 10 minutes removing foam as it rises to the surface. Strain through cheesecloth.

Soften gelatin in water and stir into hot stock. Add lemon juice. Chill until mixture begins to thicken.

Remove bones and skin from halibut and flake fish into pieces. Stir into thickened fish stock. Add green pepper, pimiento, black olives, parsley and chives. Pour into ring mold and chill overnight. Fill center with potato salad garnished with chives. Serves 8.

2 1/2 cups cooked chicken, diced
1 cup celery, finely chopped
1 cup white grapes, sliced
1/2 cup toasted almonds, slivered
2 Tbsp parsley, minced
1 tsp salt
1 1/2 Tbsp unflavored gelatin
4 Tbsp water
1/2 cup hot chicken stock
1 cup mayonnaise
1/2 cup heavy cream, whipped

In a bowl combine chicken, celery, grapes, almonds, parsley and salt.

Soften gelatin in water and dissolve in hot chicken stock. Cool until mixture begins to thicken. Stir into mayonnaise; fold in whipped cream.

Combine with salad ingredients and pour into mold. Serves 8.

3 10 1/2-oz cans chicken consommé
1 cup water
1 onion, sliced
2 stalks celery, sliced
2 Tbsp unflavored gelatin
1/2 cup water
2 hard-cooked eggs, sliced
stuffed green olives, sliced
4 cooked chicken breasts, boned and
  skinned
1 1/2 cups cooked ham, diced
1 hard-cooked egg, diced
1/2 cup celery, finely chopped
1/4 cup green onions, finely chopped
2 Tbsp pimiento, finely chopped

Heat chicken consommé with water and add onion and celery. Cover and simmer 10 minutes. Strain.

Soften gelatin in 1/2 cup cold water and stir into hot consommé to dissolve. Cool until aspic begins to thicken. Coat an ice cold mold with aspic and chill. Decorate bottom of mold with egg and olive slices first dipped in aspic; place them in a design on sides and bottom of mold. Add another layer of aspic and chill. Line mold with thinly sliced chicken breasts; spoon over more aspic and chill.

In a bowl, combine ham, egg, celery, green onions and pimiento with remaining aspic and fill the mold. Chill until firm.

Serve with 1/2 cup mayonnaise combined with 1/2 cup sour cream and chopped chives. Serves 8 to 10.

1 1/2 **Tbsp unflavored gelatin**
1/4 cup cold water
1/2 cup hot water
1 1/2 cups sour cream
1/2 cup tomato catsup
1/2 tsp salt
1/2 tsp dill weed
2 cups cooked shrimp, diced

Soften gelatin in cold water and dissolve in hot water. Cool until mixture begins to thicken. Add sour cream, catsup, salt and dill weed. Stir in shrimp and pour into mold. Chill until firm.

Unmold and garnish with shrimp. Makes 6 servings.

4 cups cooked chicken, ground
1 cup cooked rice
1/2 cup celery, finely chopped
1 Tbsp parsley, chopped
2 eggs, beaten
1/2 cup chicken broth
1 tsp salt
1/4 tsp white pepper
2 Tbsp unflavored gelatin
1/2 cup chicken broth
1 1/2 cups hot chicken broth
1 Tbsp lemon juice

Garnish: lemon slices, pimiento flowers

Make a lemon aspic by softening gelatin in cold chicken broth and then dissolving it in hot chicken broth. Add lemon juice and chill until aspic begins to thicken. Coat round mold with aspic and chill. Place lemon slices and pimientos, cut in flower shapes, on bottom of mold and spoon a little aspic on top. Chill.

Put cold chicken ring back in mold on top of the aspic (chicken ring will be slightly shrunk). Pour remaining aspic around it. Chill until firm. Serves 8.

Combine chicken, rice, celery, parsley, eggs, chicken broth, salt and pepper. Pack into a round mold without a center tube. Place mold in hot water one third the way up the sides of the mold, and bake for 45 minutes in a 350 degree oven. Let stand 10 minutes before inverting mold. Chill.

2 Tbsp unflavored gelatin
1/2 cup cold chicken stock
1/2 cup hot chicken stock
1 cup mayonnaise
1 Tbsp Worcestershire sauce
1 tsp salt
1/2 tsp pepper
2 Tbsp grated onion
2 Tbsp vinegar
2 1-lb cans red salmon, drained and flaked
2 cups cucumber, seeded and diced
3 egg whites
1 cup heavy cream, whipped

Soften gelatin in cold chicken stock and dissolve it in hot chicken stock. Cool until mixture begins to thicken. Add mayonnaise, Worcestershire sauce, salt, pepper, onion and vinegar, beating until smooth. Refrigerate 1 hour.

Beat gelatin-mayonnaise mixture again and stir in salmon and cucumber. Whip egg whites until stiff and fold into souffle with whipped cream. Pour into mold and chill until firm.

Garnish with cucumber slices and baby shrimp. Serves 10 to 12.

2 Tbsp unflavored gelatin
1/2 cup cold water
2 cups cooked ham, finely chopped
2 cups tomato juice
2 cups beef consommé
1 tsp paprika
2 cups heavy cream, whipped
salt to taste

Soften gelatin in cold water and heat over hot water until it is dissolved. Add gelatin to ham, and stir in tomato juice, beef consommé and paprika. Chill in refrigerator until it thickens. Fold in whipped cream and flavor with salt to taste. Pour into large mold or individual molds and chill until firm.

Garnish with marinated artichoke hearts and hard-cooked egg slices. Serves 10 to 12.

1 onion, thinly sliced
1 bay leaf
1/2 tsp thyme
1 sprig celery leaves
2 sprigs parsley
6 cups water
1 1/2 lb fresh shrimp (small-size)
2 slices raw carrot
2 peppercorns
2 Tbsp unflavored gelatin
1 1/2 cups shrimp stock, strained
1/2 cup dry sherry

Garnish: hard-cooked egg wedges, green olives, radish roses

In a saucepan combine onion, bay leaf, thyme, celery leaves and parsley with water. Simmer for 15 minutes. Add unshelled shrimp and boil for 5 minutes. Shell and de-vein shrimp.

Cut two small slices of carrot to make eyes for the fish in the mold. Pierce the center of each small carrot slice, then insert a peppercorn in the hole to simulate the pupil of the eye. The carrot slices are laid in the places indicated for eyes in the fish mold.

The cold cooked shrimp are arranged on the bottom of the mold in the pattern of scales to carry out the fish design. Soften gelatin in 1 1/2 cups cold strained shrimp stock which has been combined with 1/2 cup dry sherry. Heat over hot water until gelatin is dissolved. Cool until stock begins to thicken, and pour into fish mold. Chill until firm.

Unmold and garnish with hard-cooked egg wedges, green olives and radish roses. Serve with mayonnaise flavored with chopped green pepper, watercress and parsley. Serves 6.

1 Tbsp unflavored gelatin
2 Tbsp cold water
2 cups hot chicken stock
1 Tbsp grated onion
1/2 tsp salt
1/4 tsp white pepper
1 cup celery, diced
2 cups cold, cooked turkey, diced
2 pimientos, chopped
1 1/2 cups sugar
3/4 cup water
4 cups fresh cranberries
1 stick cinnamon, 2 inches long
6 whole cloves
1 orange rind, grated
2 Tbsp unflavored gelatin
2 Tbsp cold water
1/2 cup apples, peeled and diced
1/2 cup chopped walnuts

Soften gelatin in cold water and dissolve in hot chicken stock. Add grated onion, salt, and pepper. Cool until stock begins to thicken. Fold in celery, turkey and pimientos. Fill the bottom of a large mold with the turkey mixture and chill in refrigerator until firm.

Meanwhile, combine sugar and water in a saucepan and boil for a few minutes. Add cranberries, cinnamon, cloves and orange rind. Simmer until cranberry skins pop open. Press cranberries through a sieve. Soften gelatin in cold water and dissolve it in hot cranberry mixture. Cool until mixture almost thickens. Stir in apples and walnuts. Pour cranberries on top of turkey in the mold and chill until firm.

Serve with creamy mayonnaise lightly seasoned with horseradish. Serves 8.

1   1/2 Tbsp unflavored gelatin
1/2 cup cold chicken stock
1 1/2 cups hot chicken stock

Garnishes: hard-cooked egg slices, black olives, cucumber slices

2 Tbsp unflavored gelatin
1/4 cup cold water
1 1/2 cups mayonnaise
1 Tbsp Dijon-style mustard
1 Tbsp Worcestershire sauce
1/2 tsp tarragon
1/2 tsp chervil
2 Tbsp chives, chopped
1/2 cup cooked shrimp, diced
1/2 cup cooked lobster, diced
1 cup cooked crab meat,
boned and flaked

Decorate bottom of mold with egg slices, black olives and cucumber slices in an attractive design; spoon aspic on top and chill.

Soften gelatin in cold chicken stock. Dissolve in hot chicken stock. Chill until stock begins to thicken. Coat a mold with the chicken aspic. Chill.

Soften gelatin in cold water and dissolve over hot water. Stir into mayonnaise and add mustard, Worcestershire sauce, tarragon, chervil and chives. Combine with shrimp, lobster and crab meat. Fill mold with this seafood combination and chill until firm. Unmold and serve with Green Goddess dressing. Serves 6 to 8.

3/4 lb sweetbreads
2 Tbsp lemon juice
1/2 tsp salt
2 ribs celery
1/4 cup onion, chopped
peppercorns, 2 or 3
1 Tbsp unflavored gelatin
1/4 cup cold sweetbreads stock
1/4 cup hot sweetbreads stock
1 cup heavy cream, whipped
Juice of 1/2 lemon
1 Tbsp green onions, minced
1 Tbsp celery, finely chopped
2 Tbsp green pepper, finely chopped
1/2 tsp salt
1/4 tsp pepper
1/4 tsp paprika

Wash sweetbreads in cold running water. Pour 4 cups of water in a saucepan and add lemon juice, salt, celery, onion and peppercorns. Bring to a boil and add sweetbreads. Simmer for 20 minutes. Put sweetbreads in cold water for 15 minutes until they are firm enough to handle. Remove skin and membrane. Strain and reserve stock. Break sweetbreads into small pieces.

Soften gelatin in 1/4 cup cold sweetbreads stock. Heat another 1/4 cup of stock and stir in gelatin and dissolve. Cool mixture until it thickens. Fold in whipped cream. Fold in sweetbreads, lemon juice, green onion, celery, green pepper and season with salt, pepper and paprika. Pour into mold, or individual molds, and chill until firm.

Serve with mayonnaise. Serves 4.

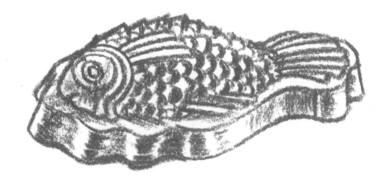

1 1/2 Tbsp unflavored gelatin
1/4 cup cold water
1 1/2 cups mayonnaise
2 cups crab meat, boned and flaked
1 cup celery, finely chopped
1 Tbsp parsley, chopped
1 Tbsp chives, chopped
1/2 tsp tarragon

Garnish: hard cooked egg wedges, baby shrimp, parsley

Soak gelatin in cold water and dissolve it over hot water. Stir gelatin into mayonnaise and combine with crab meat, celery, parsley, chives and tarragon. Pack into mold and chill in refrigerator.

Unmold and garnish with hard cooked egg wedges, baby shrimp and parsley. Serve with Russian dressing. Serves 4.

Soften gelatin in 1/2 cup of the cold chicken stock. Heat remaining stock in top of double boiler and add salt, pepper, onion and paprika. Beat egg yolks in a bowl, and add a little of the hot stock, stirring continuously. Stir egg mixture into double boiler and cook over hot water until smooth and thick. Remove from stove, stir in gelatin and cool until mixture thickens. Fold in nuts, chicken and whipped cream. Turn into mold and chill until firm.

A chicken aspic mold would be most appropriate for this dish.

Serves 8 to 10.

1   1/2 Tbsp unflavored gelatin
3 cups chicken stock
1 tsp salt
1/2 tsp pepper
1 Tbsp onion, grated
1/8 tsp paprika
3 egg yolks
1/2 cup toasted almonds, chopped
3 cups cooked chicken, finely chopped
1 cup heavy cream, whipped

2 Tbsp unflavored gelatin
1/4 cup cold water
2 egg yolks
1 tsp salt
1 tsp Dijon-style mustard
1/4 tsp paprika
3/4 cup milk
1/3 cup lemon juice
1 Tbsp butter
2 cups tuna fish, drained and flaked
1 hard-cooked egg, finely chopped
1 cup mayonnaise
2 egg whites
1 Tbsp chives, chopped

Soften gelatin in water. Beat egg yolks until they're light and lemon colored. Add salt, mustard and paprika, milk and lemon juice. Place in top of double boiler and cook over hot, but not boiling water, stirring constantly, until mixture thickens. Add butter and gelatin and stir until gelatin dissolves.

Chill until mixture begins to thicken, and fold in tuna fish, hard-cooked eggs, mayonnaise and beaten egg whites. Top with chives and lightly stir. Pour into shell molds and chill until firm. Serves 6.

1 10 1/2-oz can cream-of-chicken soup
1 can water
2 Tbsp unflavored gelatin
3/4 cup cold water
1/3 cup mayonnaise
1/2 cup heavy cream, whipped
1 1/2 cups cooked turkey, minced
1/3 cup stuffed green olives, sliced
1 stalk celery, thinly sliced
2 Tbsp green onions, minced
2 Tbsp pimiento, chopped
1 Tbsp lemon juice
1/2 tsp salt
1/4 tsp paprika

Heat soup in a saucepan with water.

Soften gelatin in cold water and stir into hot soup to dissolve. Cool until aspic thickens and fold in mayonnaise and blend. Fold in whipped cream, turkey, green olives, celery, green onions, and pimiento. Stir in lemon juice, salt and paprika. Pour into mold or individual molds and chill.

Makes 6 servings.

1 1/2 Tbsp unflavored gelatin
1/2 cup dry white wine
2 cups chicken consommé
1 Tbsp curry powder
1 cup mayonnaise
2 Tbsp green onions, finely chopped
1 cup celery, finely sliced
1 Tbsp pimiento, finely chopped
1 tsp salt
3 hard-cooked eggs, chopped
1/3 cup stuffed green olives, sliced
3 cups cooked lean lamb, cut in small cubes
2 cups cooked potatoes, peeled and diced
4 Tbsp green onions, chopped
1 tsp salt
1/2 tsp pepper
Tart french dressing

Soften gelatin in wine.

Heat 1 cup chicken consommé with curry powder and add gelatin. Stir until dissolved. Add remaining cup chicken consommé and chill until aspic thickens. Fold in mayonnaise. Stir in green onions, celery, pimiento, salt, eggs and olives. Pour into ring mold and chill until firm.

Unmold on a bed of greens and fill the center with the following lamb salad:

In a bowl, combine lamb, potatoes, onions, salt and pepper. Toss salad with a good tart french dressing, using about 3 or 4 Tbsp of dressing. Serves 8.

The following garnishes dress up a party dish with a festive note of color and design. Use them as a tasty accent.

37

Decorative Garnishes

for

Entrees and Salads

Tomato slices dipped in chopped parsley or dill
Sprigs of parsley or watercress
Whole mushrooms stuffed with deviled ham
Fresh broccoli buds
Lettuce, endive or Romaine
Lemon slices dipped in parsley
Sliced stuffed olives
Hard-cooked egg wedges
Cherry tomatoes stuffed with cottage cheese
Chopped aspic
Mayonnaise or cream cheese squeezed through pastry tube
Capers
Pickles
Pearl onions
Cooked carrots or beets cut into fanciful shapes
Pineapple slices

Large strawberries or raspberries
Melon balls
Dilled cucumbers
Orange slices or grapefruit sections
Pitted dates
Prunes stuffed with cream cheese
Marinated artichoke hearts
Canned asparagus tips
Cranberries
Cream cheese balls dipped in chopped walnuts
Radish roses

SHAPELY SALADS

The following is a basic recipe for fruit salad aspic to help you create your own salads. Vary the amount of sugar to suit your taste and to suit the purpose of the aspic—whether it's served as a salad or as a dessert.

1 Tbsp unflavored gelatin
1/2 cup cold water
1 cup boiling water or fruit juice
4 to 6 Tbsp sugar
1/4 tsp salt
1/4 cup lemon juice
1   1/2 cups prepared drained fruit

Soften gelatin in cold water and dissolve in hot water or fruit juice. Add sugar, salt and lemon juice. Cool until gelatin begins to thicken and add prepared, drained fruit.

Incidentally, the only fresh fruit that does not fare well in the refrigerator is fresh pineapple. Always use canned pineapple or fresh pineapple that has been cooked.

1 3-oz package lemon-flavored gelatin
1 3/4 cup hot orange juice
1 1/2 Tbsp lemon juice
1/2 tsp salt
3 ripe peeled persimmons, pureed

Garnish: sour cream and slivered almonds

Dissolve lemon-flavored gelatin in hot orange juice. Add lemon juice and salt. Chill in refrigerator until gelatin thickens. Fold in pureed persimmons and pour into crown mold. Chill until firm.

Serve with sour cream and slivered almonds. Serves 6.

1 12-oz package frozen peaches, defrosted
1 12-oz package frozen raspberries, defrosted
1/4 cup frozen lemonade, defrosted
2 Tbsp unflavored gelatin
1/2 cup cold water
1 cup boiling water
1/4 tsp salt
1 Tbsp sugar
1 4-oz can frozen orange juice, defrosted
1 large banana, diced
1/2 cup seeded green grapes
1/4 cup walnut halves
1/2 cup pitted dates, sliced

Reserve juice from thawed peaches and raspberries. Pour lemonade over peaches.

Soften gelatin in cold water then dissolve in hot water. Add salt, sugar, orange juice, peach juice and raspberry juice to gelatin. Chill until mixture begins to thicken, then fold in peaches, raspberries, banana, grapes, walnuts and dates. Pour into a large fruit-design mold and chill until firm.

Serve with creamy mayonnaise dressing. Serves 8.

2 Tbsp unflavored gelatin
1/2 cup cold water
1 1/2 cups boiling water
6 Tbsp lime juice
1 Tbsp grated onion
2 tsp salt
Dash of Tabasco sauce
3 cups avocados, mashed
3/4 cup mayonnaise

Soften gelatin in cold water and then dissolve in boiling water. Add lemon juice, grated onion, salt and a lively dash of Tabasco. Chill until aspic thickens.

Stir in mashed avocados and fold in mayonnaise. Pour into mold and chill until firm.

A clover leaf mold from Mexico shapes this dish into a decorative attraction for your buffet table. Serves 8.

1 Tbsp unflavored gelatin
1/4 cup cold water
1 1/2 cups beef bouillon
1 Tbsp lemon juice
3 hard-cooked eggs, sliced
2 cans (3 1/4 oz each) boneless, skinless
    sardines
1 Tbsp green onions, finely chopped

Soften gelatin in cold water. Heat beef bouillon and add lemon juice and gelatin. Stir until gelatin is dissolved. Chill until aspic thickens. Use one-fourth of the aspic to coat a mold and chill until set.

Arrange sliced eggs in a decorative pattern on top of aspic. Cut sardines in 1 1/2 inch lengths and alternate with eggs in a pattern. Sprinkle onions over the top. Spoon over remaining aspic and chill until firm.

Unmold and garnish with lemon slices dipped in chopped parsley. Serves 6.

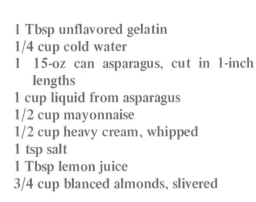

1 Tbsp unflavored gelatin
1/4 cup cold water
1   15-oz can asparagus, cut in 1-inch
    lengths
1 cup liquid from asparagus
1/2 cup mayonnaise
1/2 cup heavy cream, whipped
1 tsp salt
1 Tbsp lemon juice
3/4 cup blanced almonds, slivered

Drain liquid from asparagus and add sufficient water to make 1 cup. Heat liquid and add gelatin; stir until dissolved.

Chill until mixture begins to thicken. Fold in mayonnaise, whipped cream, salt and lemon juice. Fold in asparagus and almonds. Pour into mold and chill.

Serve with mayonnaise flavored with lemon juice. Serves 8.

Soften gelatin in cold water.

Black Cherry, Pineapple, and Walnut Aspic

1 Tbsp unflavored gelatin
1/2 cup cold water
1 cup juice from black cherries
2 Tbsp sugar
1/8 tsp salt
1/4 cup lemon juice
1 cup pitted black cherries
1/2 cup pineapple tidbits
1/3 cup chopped walnuts

Soften gelatin in cold water.

Heat juice and water to a boiling point and dissolve gelatin. Add sugar, salt and lemon juice and cool until aspic thickens. Stir in black cherries, pineapple and almonds and pour into a fruit mold and chill until set.

Serve with a creamy dressing. Serves 6.

1   8-oz can baby peas
1   8-oz can carrots, diced
1   8-oz can green beans, cut in half
1   8-oz can small pickled beets
1 1/2 Tbsp unflavored gelatin
1/2 cup cold water
1 1/2 cups mayonnaise
1 1/2 Tbsp unflavored gelatin
1/2 cup cold chicken stock
2 cups hot chicken stock

Drain vegetables.

Soften gelatin in cold water, dissolve over hot water; stir into mayonnaise. Combine vegetables and mayonnaise.

Soften second 1 1/2 tablespoons of gelatin in cold chicken stock and dissolve in hot chicken stock. Cool until aspic thickens.

Coat individual molds with chicken aspic and chill in refrigerator. Fill with vegetable mixture and chill.

Spoon out a top layer of chicken aspic over the vegetables and chill in refrigerator until firm. Serves 8.

2 Tbsp unflavored gelatin
1/2 cup cold water
3 1/2 cups canned prune juice
4 cups canned prunes, pitted and
    coarsely chopped
1/2 cup chopped walnuts
2 Tbsp lemon juice

Soften gelatin in cold water.

Heat prune juice and dissolve gelatin. Cool until mixture begins to thicken. Add prunes, walnuts, and lemon juice. Pour into ring mold and chill until firm.

Unmold and fill center with cream cheese beaten with light cream to the consistency of whipped cream. Sprinkle top with grated lemon.

Try this with turkey, chicken or ham. Serves 12.

3 large cucumbers, peeled and seeded
1 Tbsp unflavored gelatin
1 tsp salt
2 Tbsp grated onion
1/2 tsp paprika
1/2 tsp white pepper
1 1/2 cups cottage cheese, drained and sieved

Grate cucumbers and strain, reserving juice. Soften gelatin in cucumber juice and dissolve gelatin over a pan of hot water. Season mixture with salt, grated onion, paprika and white pepper. Cool until mixture begins to thicken. Stir in cucumbers and fold in cottage cheese which has been put through a sieve. Mix well and turn into a melon mold.

Chill until firm and unfold on a bed of watercress.

Serve with mayonnaise. Serves 6.

2 Tbsp unflavored gelatin
1/4 cup cold water
1 cup hot water
12 oz cream cheese, softened
1 cup Blue Cheese, softened
2 tsp Worcestershire sauce
1/4 cup parsley, finely chopped
1 tsp salt
1 tsp paprika
1 1/2 cups heavy cream, whipped

Soften gelatin in cold water and dissolve it in hot water.

Combine cream cheese with Blue Cheese and blend well with Worcestershire, parsley, salt and paprika. Stir into gelatin and chill until it thickens. Fold in whipped cream and pour into mold and chill until firm.

This is an ideal hors d'oeuvre to serve with crackers. (Cheddar cheese may be used in place of Blue Cheese for a variation.) Serves 8 to 10.

Raspberry Wreath

2 10-oz packages frozen raspberries, defrosted
3 1/2 cups raspberry juice
2 3-oz packages raspberry-flavored gelatin
1 cup sour cream
1 10-oz package frozen sliced peaches, defrosted

Thaw raspberries and reserve liquid. Add sufficient water to make 3 1/2 cups of liquid. Heat 2 cups liquid to boiling point; add gelatin and stir to dissolve. Add remaining liquid and chill until mixture begins to thicken. Fold in drained raspberries and pour half into the bottom of a mold. Chill in refrigerator until firm.

Remove from refrigerator and cover with sour cream and a layer of drained sliced peaches. Cover this with remaining raspberry gelatin and return to refrigerator. Chill until firm.

Unmold and garnish with cream cheese balls dusted with finely chopped pecans. Serves 6.

2 1/2 Tbsp unflavored gelatin
1/2 cup water
1 No. 2 1/2 can peach halves
2 cups peach juice
1 1/2 cups sugar
3/4 cup lemon juice
3 Tbsp lime juice
1 8-oz package cream cheese
1 Tbsp mayonnaise
finely chopped walnuts

boil. Add gelatin and stir until dissolved. Remove from stove and add lemon juice and lime juice. Measure liquid and add sufficient water to make 4 cups. Chill until liquid begins to thicken.

Soften cream cheese with mayonnaise and shape into individual 1-inch balls. Roll balls in chopped walnuts and place inside peach halves. Allow 1 peach half per serving.

Place stuffed peach halves in individual molds and pour 1/2 cup of thickened gelatin mixture over each mold. Chill until firm. Serves 8.

Soften gelatin in water.

Drain canned peaches and reserve juice. Add sufficient water to juice to make 2 cups. Pour peach juice and sugar into a saucepan and bring to a

2 Tbsp unflavored gelatin
1/2 cup cold water
2 1/2 cups pineapple juice
3/4 cup mint jelly
3 drops mint flavoring
3 drops green food coloring
1 cup sour cream
1 1-lb 4-oz can crushed pineapple, drained

Soak gelatin in cold water.

Heat pineapple juice and add gelatin; stir until dissolved. Add mint jelly and dissolve. Remove from stove and cool until pineapple-gelatin thickens. Beat in mint flavoring and green food coloring. Fold in sour cream and pineapple. Blend well, and pour into clover leaf mold. Chill until firm.

Garnish with mint leaves. Serves 6.

1 Tbsp unflavored gelatin
1 Tbsp sugar
1 tsp salt
1/8 tsp pepper
1/2 cup cold water
1 1/4 cup water
1/4 cup vinegar
1 Tbsp lemon juice
1/4 cup chopped green onions
1 cup shredded raw spinach
1 cup chopped celery
1/4 cup shredded raw carrots

Mix gelatin, sugar, salt and pepper in 1/2 cup water.

Heat 1 1/4 cups of water and stir in gelatin mixture. Add vinegar and lemon juice. Chill until mixture begins to thicken. Fold in green onions, spinach, celery and raw carrots. Pour into mold and chill until firm.

Unmold and garnish with marinated artichoke hearts, tomatoes and cucumber slices. Serve with French dressing. Serves 6.

6 hard-cooked eggs, finely chopped
6 green onions, finely chopped
6 sprigs watercress leaves, finely
    chopped
1 stalk celery, finely chopped
3/4 tsp salt
1/4 tsp pepper
1/4 tsp nutmeg
1/4 tsp powdered cloves
2 Tbsp sweet pickle, finely chopped
1/4 cup canned deviled ham
1 tsp Worcestershire sauce
1/4 cup French Dressing
2 Tbsp capers
1 Tbsp unflavored gelatin
1/2 cup cold water
1 Tbsp lemon juice
1 cup dry white wine

Combine finely chopped eggs, onions, watercress, celery, salt, pepper, nutmeg, cloves, sweet pickle, ham and Worcestershire sauce. Stir in French Dressing and capers.

Soften gelatin in cold water and lemon juice.

Heat wine and dissolve gelatin in wine. Cool until mixture begins to thicken. Stir in egg salad and pour into ring mold.

Unmold and fill ring with chicken or tuna fish salad. Serves 8.

1 3-oz package lemon-flavored gelatin
2 cups boiling water
1/2 cup heavy cream, whipped
1 cup canned, crushed pineapple
1 cup chopped walnuts
1/4 cup stuffed green olives, sliced
1 cup American cheese, grated

Dissolve package of lemon-flavored gelatin in boiling water.

Chill until mixture begins to thicken. Whip gelatin and fold in whipped cream, pineapple, walnuts, stuffed green olives and American cheese.

Pour into mold and chill until firm.

Serve with creamy salad dressing. Serves 6 to 8.

1 1/2 Tbsp unflavored gelatin
1/4 cup cold water
1/2 cup boiling water
1 1/2 cups grapefruit juice
2 Tbsp lemon juice
1 Tbsp sugar
1/2 tsp salt
1 cup canned grapefruit sections, coarsely cut
1 cup cucumber, seeded and finely chopped

Soften gelatin in cold water. Dissolve in hot water. Add grapefruit juice, lemon juice, sugar and salt.

Chill until mixture begins to thicken. Fold in grapefruit sections and cucumber. Pour into fruit design mold and chill until firm.

Serve with sour cream mayonnaise dressing. Serves 6.

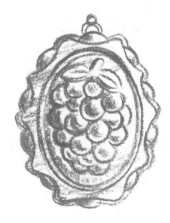

1 cup cup canned beets, drained and
   diced
1 3-oz package lemon-flavored gelatin
1 cup boiling water
3/4 cup beet juice
3 Tbsp vinegar
1/2 tsp salt
2 tsp grated onion
1 Tbsp prepared horseradish
3/4 cup celery, diced

Dissolve gelatin in boiling water. Add beet juice, vinegar, salt, onion, gelatin and horseradish. Chill until gelatin thickens. Fold in beets and celery.

Drain beets and reserve juice.

Pour into a festive mold such as one of the Mexican star, diamond, or crown-and-points molds. Serves 6 to 8.

1 Tbsp unflavored gelatin
2 Tbsp cold water
1/2 cup boiling water
1 Tbsp lemon juice
1 tsp Worcestershire sauce
2 Tbsp mayonnaise
2 cups sour cream
1/8 tsp dry mustard
4 1/2 oz black caviar or lumpfish caviar

Garnish: paprika, lemon wedges

Soften gelatin in cold water and then dissolve it in hot water. Cool. Add lemon juice, Worcestershire, and mayonnaise. Fold in sour cream. Stir in mustard and caviar or lumpfish. Pour into individual molds or single mold. Chill until firm.

Unmold and garnish with paprika and lemon wedges. This makes an original hors d'oeuvre. Serves 8.

4 cups fresh cranberries
1 1/2 cups sugar
1 cup water
1 1/2 Tbsp unflavored gelatin
1/4 cup cold water
2 Tbsp lime or lemon juice
2/3 cup walnuts, coarsely chopped
1 cup celery, diced

Pick over and wash cranberries.

Boil sugar and water for 5 minutes. Add berries and cook slowly without stirring until berries break open in approximately 5 minutes.

Soften gelatin in cold water and dissolve in hot cranberry sauce. Add lime or lemon juice. Cool until mixture begins to thicken. Add walnuts and celery. Pour into ring mold and chill until firm.

Unmold on a bed of watercress or lettuce and serve with a creamy salad dressing. Center may be filled with cottage cheese whipped with a little sour cream. Serves 6 to 8.

1   1-lb 3-oz can blue plums
1 3/4 cups plum juice
1   3-oz package cherry-flavored gelatin
1/4 tsp cinnamon
1/8 tsp ground cloves
1/8 tsp nutmeg

Drain plums and reserve juice. Add sufficient water to juice to make 1 3/4 cups of liquid. Heat 1 cup of plum liquid to boiling point, add cherry-flavored gelatin and dissolve. Add remaining liquid. Chill until mixture thickens.

Pit plums and puree in blender. Pour pureed plums into gelatin and add cinnamon, cloves, and nutmeg Pour into mold and chill until firm.

This may be served as a salad; or, as a side dish with a meat course. Serves 6.

2 pints fresh blueberries
1/2 cup orange juice
1/2 cup sugar
2   3-oz packages lemon-flavored gelatin
1 cup boiling water
3/4 cup cold water
1/4 cup blackberry brandy
2 cups sour cream
1 Tbsp lemon rind, grated
1/2 tsp nutmeg
1/2 tsp cinnamon

In a saucepan combine 1 pint of blueberries, orange juice and sugar. Bring to a boil and cool.

In another saucepan dissolve gelatin in 1 cup boiling water and add 3/4 cup cold water. Cool and add blackberry brandy. Mix with partially cooked blueberries, sour cream, lemon rind, nutmeg and cinnamon. Stir in remaining pint of uncooked blueberries. Pour into mold and chill until firm.

Serve with sour cream. Serves 8.

2 3-oz packages lemon-flavored gelatin
2 cups boiling water
1 1-lb 1-oz can of apricots
1 cup sour cream
1 pint vanilla ice cream, softened

Dissolve gelatin in hot water, then cool.

Drain apricots. Puree apricots in a blender and add to gelatin.

Whip sour cream and vanilla ice cream together and fold into apricots.

Pour into a mold and chill until firm. Serves 8.

Keep your punch bowl chilled with an ice garland of fruit that floats!

Select a ring mold that will fit easily into your punch bowl. Fill ring half full of water and put in freezer. When water is frozen, remove and arrange slices of gaily colored fruit and decorative leaves around the top of the ice. Carefully pour a small amount of water around the fruit and leaves, just enough to anchor them to the ice ring. Return to freezer, and freeze long enough for the fruit and leaves to adhere to the ice. If they do not, add a little more water and return to freezer.

To unmold, dip mold quickly in hot water.

Float ring, fruit side up, in punch bowl.

We recommend the use of vivid fruits such as peaches, dark cherries, strawberries, or slices of pineapple, lemon, or lime. Any small, pretty leaves, such as lemon leaves, are appropriate. For a festive Christmas punch bowl, try red and green cherries on your molded fruit wreath.

DECORATIVE DESSERTS

And now for the finale of your dinner party, the dessert course! Like all good finales, it must be grand. This is the moment that climaxes your dinner and insures your reputation as a culinary genius. Your dessert has to be nothing short of a high-caloried masterpiece.

There are many kinds of molded desserts but none are more elegant or spectacular than the frozen mousse and parfait. The mousse, or bombe, as it's frequently called, has a whipped cream base and is often combined with gelatin or eggs, and flavored with fruit or chocolate or coffee. On the other hand, the parfait is made with beaten egg whites over which a hot syrup is poured. This is then combined with whipped cream. Both of these frozen ambrosias are successfully molded.

At one time mousses, or bombes, were traditionally served in a spherical "bomb" shape, but today they're molded in any design to suit your fancy. There are many charming ice cream molds you can use for mousses or parfaits–or most regular molds will do. The only special requirement for making frozen desserts is that the mold be filled to the very top and covered with a buttered, heavy wax paper before sealing with a tight lid, or foil paper tied around the top to keep the mold waterproof. These molded confections are unmolded the same as aspics: by quickly dipping the bottom of the mold in hot water, and reversing onto a chilled plate.

In instances where you're making an elaborate frozen dessert combining two or three different kinds of commercial ice cream with a whipped cream or mousse filling, it's best to use a cassata mold with a rounded top, or a charlotte mold. Place the mold in a bed of ice and work as fast as you can in evenly spreading the outside layers of ice cream. If the ice cream softens too much in the process, return to the freezer to harden before proceeding.

Incidentally, if you want to mold commercial ice cream, simply soften the ice cream, stir in a few flavorful touches of your own, pack it into a mold and refreeze.

In the following chapter we've also included molded desserts that are chilled but not frozen—such as the luscious sweet souffles, charlottes and cremes.

Raspberry Parfait

1 qt raspberries, crushed
3/4 cup water
1 cup sugar
3 egg whites
1/4 tsp salt
2 cups heavy cream, whipped

Crush raspberries and strain them through a cheesecloth.

In a saucepan combine water and sugar and cook until the syrup is sufficiently thick to spin a thread when a drop is poured from a spoon.

Whip egg whites until stiff and pour syrup over them in a slow steady stream. Keep whipping until cool. Fold in crushed berries. Fold in whipped cream.

Freeze parfait in an ice cream mold, preferably of a fanciful design such as a rooster ice cream mold. Serves 6.

1 1/2 tsp unflavored gelatin
1/4 cup cold water
2 cups milk
1 1/2 cups sugar
2 egg yolks, beaten
1 tsp vanilla
4 cups heavy cream, whipped
2 egg whites
1/4 tsp salt

Soften gelatin in cold water.

Heat milk and sugar in the top of a double boiler and bring to a boil. Add gelatin and stir until dissolved.

Pour a little hot milk over beaten egg yolks and stir eggs slowly into milk.

Cook in double boiler over low fire until eggs thicken slightly. Cool and add vanilla. When custard thickens fold in whipped cream.

Beat egg whites together with salt and fold into custard.

Pour into molds and freeze. A dove ice cream mold is ideally suited to the delicate color of this mousse. Serves 10 to 12.

This is a basic vanilla mousse that can be sparked with various crushed fruits, or flavored with liqueurs. It also makes an elegant filling for a bombe when it's used with contrasting ice cream, or ices such as raspberry or pistachio.

1/2 cup glacéed or candied fruit
2 Tbsp rum
1 qt vanilla ice cream
1 1/2 pints raspberry ice
1 pint coffee ice cream
1 cup heavy cream, whipped

Garnish: glacéed cherry, citron, and whipped cream

Soak candied fruit in rum for 1/2 hour.

Line a 6-cup, dome-shaped cassatta mold with 1 pint vanilla ice cream, and over this add a layer of raspberry ice and a layer of coffee ice cream.

Stir rum-soaked fruit into the remaining pint of softened vanilla ice cream and fold in 1/2 cup whipped cream. Fill center of mold. Cover with buttered wax paper and a lid and freeze until ice cream is firm.

Half an hour before serving, unmold onto a chilled serving plate and garnish with a cherry, slices of citron, and remaining whipped cream. Return to freezer. Makes 10 servings.

1 cup fresh pineapple-pulp with juice
1 cup sugar
3/4 cup water
1/4 tsp salt
1 1/2 tsp gelatin
2 Tbsp water
3 Tbsp rum
1 cup heavy cream

Put pineapple in a blender and blend until it is of a pulpy consistency. In a saucepan combine pineapple, sugar, water and salt. Bring to a boil and simmer 6 or 7 minutes.

Soak gelatin in 2 Tbsp water. Add to pineapple mixture and chill.

Stir in rum and fold in whipped cream. Pour into a pineapple-shaped mold and freeze.

Unmold and surround with rum-soaked pineapple rings. Serves 4.

1 cup chopped marrons (chestnuts)
1/4 cup dark rum
2/3 cup sugar
1/3 cup water
5 egg yolks, well-beaten
1 1/2 cups heavy cream, whipped

Chop marrons and place in a bowl. Pour in rum and marinate marrons for several hours.

Boil sugar and water for 5 minutes and pour in a fine, steady stream over beaten egg yolks, beating constantly. Cook in the top of a double boiler until custard thickens. Chill.

Drain marrons and sprinkle 1/4 cup on the bottom of mold.

Fold whipped cream into custard and add remaining 3/4 cup of marrons.

Pour into mold, cover and freeze for several hours, or overnight. Serves 6.

1 qt fresh strawberries
1/4 cup sugar
1 Tbsp lemon juice
1 Tbsp brandy
2 cups heavy cream, whipped
1/2 cup powdered sugar

Wash and hull berries, saving a few berries for garnishing. Chop strawberries in a bowl and add sugar and lemon juice. Puree strawberries in a blender and add brandy. Fold in whipped cream sweetened with powdered sugar.

Pour into heart shaped molds.

Cover with buttered waxed paper and foil; freeze until firm.

Unmold and garnish with whole berries. Serves 6.

2 cups peaches, pureed
1 Tbsp unflavored gelatin
1/4 cup cold water
2 Tbsp lemon juice
3/4 cup sugar
2 cups heavy cream, whipped

Peel and slice sufficient peaches to make 2 cups. Put peaches into blender and blend until they are pureed.

Soak gelatin in 1/4 cup cold water for a few minutes. Stir gelatin over hot water until completely dissolved. Combine the peach puree with the gelatin, lemon juice, and sugar, then chill.

Fold in whipped cream and pour into individual peach-shaped ice cream molds and freeze until firm. Serves 6.

2 cups sour cream
1 Tbsp rum
4 Tbsp crushed macaroons
4 Tbsp sweet chocolate, melted
1/2 cup sugar
1 tsp vanilla

In a bowl, combine the sour cream, rum, crushed macaroons, melted chocolate, sugar and vanilla. Stir thoroughly.

Pour into mold and freeze. Serves 4.

1 pint fresh strawberries, washed and hulled
1/3 cup sugar
1/8 tsp salt
3 Tbsp corn syrup
1 tsp gelatin
3 Tbsp cold water
1 cup heavy cream, whipped
1/2 cup macaroons, finely crushed
1 qt vanilla ice cream

Sprinkle strawberries with sugar and let stand for 1 hour. Chop strawberries as finely as possible and stir in salt and corn syrup.

Soak gelatin in cold water. Dissolve it over a pan of hot water. Cool and add gelatin to strawberries. Fold in whipped cream and macaroons.

Line a cassatta ice cream mold or a charlotte mold with vanilla ice cream and fill with strawberry-macaroon mixture.

Cover with buttered waxed paper and cover. Freeze until firm. Garnish with whole strawberries. Serves 8.

Melon Mousse

1 Tbsp unflavored gelatin
1/4 cup cold water
2 cups ripe honeydew melon or canta-
    loupe, mashed
1/2 cup sugar
1 Tbsp lemon juice
1/2 tsp vanilla
1 cup heavy cream, whipped

Soften gelatin in cold water.

Combine mashed or crushed melon or cantaloupe, sugar, and lemon juice in a saucepan; and simmer a few minutes until sugar is melted. Stir in gelatin and chill until mixture begins to thicken. Stir in vanilla and fold in whipped cream.

Pour into melon-shaped mold and cover. Freeze until firm. Serves 6.

1 cup sugar
3/4 cup strong coffee
3 egg whites
1/4 tsp salt
1 1/2 tsp vanilla
2 cups heavy cream, whipped
3 Tbsp dark rum

Beat egg whites until stiff and add salt. Pour syrup over egg whites in a slow steady stream, beating continuously. Add vanilla and keep whipping until mixture thickens and is cool. Fold in whipped cream, and stir in rum.

Pour into molds and freeze. Serves 6.

In a saucepan combine sugar and coffee. Bring to a boil and cook syrup for 5 minutes or until syrup spins a thread when a drop is poured from a spoon. Remove from stove and cool.

6 egg yolks
1 1/2 cups dark honey, strained
3 egg whites
1 pint heavy cream, whipped

Garnish: finely chopped pistachio nuts

Beat egg yolks until light and lemon-colored. Whip in honey gradually and beat until blended.

In the top of a double boiler cook egg-honey mixture, stirring constantly, over hot, but not boiling water until it thickens. Chill.

Beat egg whites until stiff and fold into egg-honey custard. Fold in whipped cream. Pour into a mold.

Freeze until firm. Unmold and garnish with finely chopped pistachio nuts. Serves 6.

2 eggs
1/2 cup maple syrup
1 cup heavy cream, whipped
1/2 tsp salt
1/4 cup peanut brittle, finely crushed

Beat eggs until light and lemon colored.

Heat maple syrup and pour a little of the egg mixture into syrup. Beat the rest of the eggs into syrup. Heat mixture in the top of a double boiler until it thickens. Cool.

Fold in whipped cream, salt and crushed peanut brittle.

Pour into mold and freeze until firm. Serves 4.

Three inventive flavor combinations transform plain ice cream into party-specials. Thaw the ice cream sufficiently to permit the easy mixing of additional ingredients. Thereafter pour into ice cream molds and refreeze.

Marron Ice Cream

1 qt vanilla ice cream, softened
1 cup marrons, coarsely chopped
2 Tbsp sherry

Chocolate Coffee

1 qt chocolate ice cream, softened
3 Tbsp bitter chocolate, finely chopped
3 Tbsp Kahlúa

Orange-Cointreau

1 qt vanilla ice cream, softened
2 Tbsp orange peel, grated
3 Tbsp Cointreau

Chocolate Souffle

4 egg yolks
1/4 cup fine sugar
2 Tbsp Cognac, or brandy
6 oz semisweet chocolate
1 tsp instant coffee
1/4 lb sweet butter, cut in small chunks
4 egg whites, stiffly whipped

Garnish: 1/2 cup heavy cream, whipped

Beat egg yolks and sugar with a whisk, or electric beater, for 2 or 3 minutes until mixture slightly thickens. Stir in Cognac. Pour into top of a double boiler and cook over hot, but not boiling water, for 2 or 3 minutes, beating continuously until mixture is foamy and hot. Place top of double boiler in a bowl of ice and continue beating until mixture is the consistency of mayonnaise.

In a separate saucepan, melt chocolate, add coffee and stir in the butter. Cook until butter has melted and sauce is creamy.

Slowly blend chocolate sauce into the egg mixture. Fold in whipped egg whites and pour into ring mold, or individual dessert molds and chill until firm.

Top with whipped cream before serving. Serves 6 to 8.

1 Tbsp unflavored gelatin
1/4 cup lemon juice
3 eggs, beaten
3/4 cup sugar
1 Tbsp grated lemon peel
1 cup heavy cream, whipped

Garnish: orange slices and whipped cream

Soften gelatin in lemon juice. Set bowl over hot water until gelatin is dissolved.

In a separate bowl, beat eggs until they're light and frothy. Beat in sugar, stirring continuously until mixture is thick. Add lemon peel. Combine whipped cream with gelatin-lemon juice mixture, and fold into eggs.

Pour into molds and chill overnight.

Unmold and garnish with mandarin orange slices and whipped cream. Serves 4.

1 Tbsp unflavored gelatin
2 Tbsp cold water
1/2 cup scalded milk
4 egg yolks
1/4 cup sugar
1/8 tsp salt
3/4 cup black walnuts, ground
1 tsp vanilla
2 cups heavy cream, whipped

In a bowl, beat egg yolks until light and pale yellow, adding sugar and salt. Beat in a little hot milk into the egg mixture, and then stir eggs gradually into top of double boiler, stirring continuously until custard begins to thicken. Stir in gelatin and add black walnuts and vanilla. Chill.

Soak gelatin in cold water.

Heat milk in top of double boiler.

Fold in whipping cream and pour into mold and chill until firm. Garnish with whipped cream and whole black walnuts. Serves 8.

2 Tbsp unflavored gelatin
1/4 cup cold water
2 cups milk, scalded
1/2 cup sugar
4 egg yolks
1 Tbsp brandy
4 egg whites
1/8 tsp salt
2 cups heavy cream, whipped
18 Lady fingers

Garnish: Maraschino cherries and whipped cream

Soften gelatin in cold water and dissolve it in scalded milk. Stir in sugar.

Beat egg yolks until light and pale yellow. Gradually add a little of the gelatin-milk mixture to egg yolks, and then pour mixture into top of double boiler. Cook custard over hot, but not boiling water until it begins to thicken. Cool. Add brandy.

Whip egg whites until stiff, add salt, whipped cream, and fold lightly into custard. Line a charlotte mold with Lady fingers, decoratively arranged on the bottom and standing upright against inside wall of mold.

Pour in the custard and chill in refrigerator.

Unmold and garnish with Maraschino cherries and whipped cream. Serves 10 to 12.

1 Tbsp unflavored gelatin
1/4 cup cold water
2 tsp instant coffee
1/2 cup cold water
4 egg yolks
1/2 cup sugar
1/2 tsp salt
1 tsp vanilla
4 egg whites
1/2 cup sugar
1 cup heavy cream, whipped

Soften gelatin in water.

Dissolve instant coffee in 1/2 cup cold water.

Beat egg yolks until light and pale yellow. Mix with coffee, sugar and salt. Cook in the top of a double boiler over hot, but not boiling water, until custard thickens. Remove from heat, add gelatin—stirring until it dissolves. Add vanilla, then cool.

Beat egg whites until stiff and fold in 1/2 cup sugar.

Combine coffee custard and whipped cream and fold in egg whites. Pour in mold and chill until firm. Serves 6 to 8.

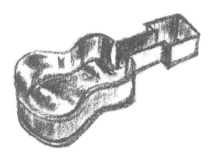

1 Tbsp unflavored gelatin
6 Tbsp sugar
2 Tbsp instant coffee
2 egg yolks
2 cups milk
1/2 tsp almond extract
2 egg whites

Garnish: whipped cream and shaved bitter chocolate

Combine gelatin, sugar and instant coffee in top of double boiler.

Beat egg yolks and blend with cold milk. Pour into double boiler. Cook over low heat until mixture thickens slightly. Remove from heat and stir in almond extract. Chill, stirring occasionally until mixture mounds a little when poured from the spoon.

Beat egg whites until stiff and fold into custard gelatin mixture. Pour into mold and chill until firm.

Garnish with whipped cream and shaved bitter chocolate. Serves 6.

1 Tbsp unflavored gelatin
1/4 cup cold water
1 cup canned fig juice
1/3 cup sugar
1/8 tsp salt
1 Tbsp lemon juice
1/8 tsp almond extract
1 cup canned figs
1 cup heavy cream, whipped

Soften gelatin in cold water.

Combine fig juice, sugar and salt in saucepan. Bring to a boiling point and simmer 3 minutes. Add gelatin and stir until dissolved. Cool until mixture begins to thicken and add lemon juice and almond extract.

Cut half the figs into slices and arrange on the bottom of mold.

Fold whipped cream into gelatin mixture. Dice remaining figs and stir into mixture. Pour over layer of figs in mold. Chill until firm.

Unmold and serve with whipped cream. Serves 6.

1 lb creamed cottage cheese
1 lb cream cheese
1 cup heavy cream
4 Tbsp honey

Garnish: fresh strawberries, or strawberry preserves and sour cream

Pass the cottage cheese through a fine strainer. Mix well with softened cream cheese, cream and honey. Pour into individual Coeur a La Creme heart-shaped molds with holes for drainage, lined with a dampened piece of cheesecloth large enough to fold over the cheese. Close the cheesecloth tightly over the mixture, packing it down with the hands.

Place the molds on a plate to drain and chill overnight.

Serve with fresh strawberries, or strawberry preserves and sour cream. Serves 12.

1 Tbsp unflavored gelatin
3/4 cup sugar
1/4 tsp salt
2 egg yolks
1/2 cup cold water
6-oz can frozen orange juice, undiluted
2 egg whites
1 cup heavy cream, whipped

Garnish: whipped cream, orange sections, strawberries

Mix gelatin, 1/2 cup sugar and salt.

Beat .egg yolk with water and stir into gelatin mixture. Cook approximately 5 minutes in double boiler over low heat, stirring constantly until gelatin dissolves, and custard slightly thickens. Remove from heat, add frozen orange juice and stir until melted. Mixture should mound slightly when poured from a spoon; if not, chill a few minutes.

Beat egg whites until stiff and add 1/4 cup sugar. Fold into whipped cream and stir into orange custard. Pour into mold and chill until firm.

Unmold and garnish with whipped cream, orange sections and whole strawberries. Serves 6.

2 Tbsp unflavored gelatin
1/4 cup sugar
1/4 tsp salt
4 egg yolks
1/2 cup water
2 10-oz packages frozen, sliced strawberries
2 Tbsp lemon juice
2 tsp grated lemon rind
8 lady fingers, split in half
4 egg whites
1/2 cup sugar
1 cup heavy cream, whipped

Mix gelatin, sugar, and salt, then place in top of a double boiler.

Beat egg yolks and water together then pour into double boiler. Add 1 package frozen strawberries and cook about 8 minutes over boiling water until gelatin is dissolved and strawberries thawed. Remove from fire and add remaining package of strawberries, lemon juice and rind. Stir until strawberries are thawed.

Chill until mixture begins to thicken.

Split lady fingers in half and stand around the edge of an 8-inch spring-form pan.

Beat egg whites until stiff, and beat in 1/2 cup sugar. Fold into strawberry-gelatin mixture. Fold in whipped cream and pour into mold. Chill until firm.

Remove from pan onto a serving dish and decorate with whipped cream and whole strawberries on top. Serves 10.

2 Tbsp unflavored gelatin
1/4 cup cold water
2 Tbsp lemon juice
4 eggs, whole
3 egg yolks
1/2 cup sugar
1 cup pureed apricots
1 Tbsp cognac, or brandy
1/2 tsp vanilla
1 cup heavy cream, whipped

Soften gelatin in cold water and lemon juice. Dissolve gelatin in a pan over hot water.

Beat whole eggs, egg yolks and sugar with an electric beater until eggs are thick and lemon-colored. Add pureed apricots to egg mixture together with cognac, vanilla, and gelatin. Fold in whipped cream and pour into mold and chill.

Unmold and decorate with whipped cream. Serves 6 to 8.

2 cups heavy cream, whipped
1 Tbsp sugar
1 tsp vanilla
1 Tbsp unflavored gelatin
1/4 cup cold water
3 cups fresh raspberries soaked in Kirsch or Cointreau

Blend whipped cream with sugar and vanilla.

Soak gelatin in cold water and stir over hot water until gelatin dissolves. Add to whipped cream, folding it in lightly. Pour into mold and chill.

Unmold and spoon over fresh raspberries soaked in Kirsch or Cointreau. Serves 6.

Index